baby shower

IN CELEBRATION OF

_____

_____

DATE

_____

CONGRATULATIONS

Congratulations on your new bundle of joy!
I am so excited for you. I hope this guest book will be
a memorable keepsake that you will cherish for years
to come. Enjoy every moment of this joyous journey!

Zady Rose
www.collectedjoys.com

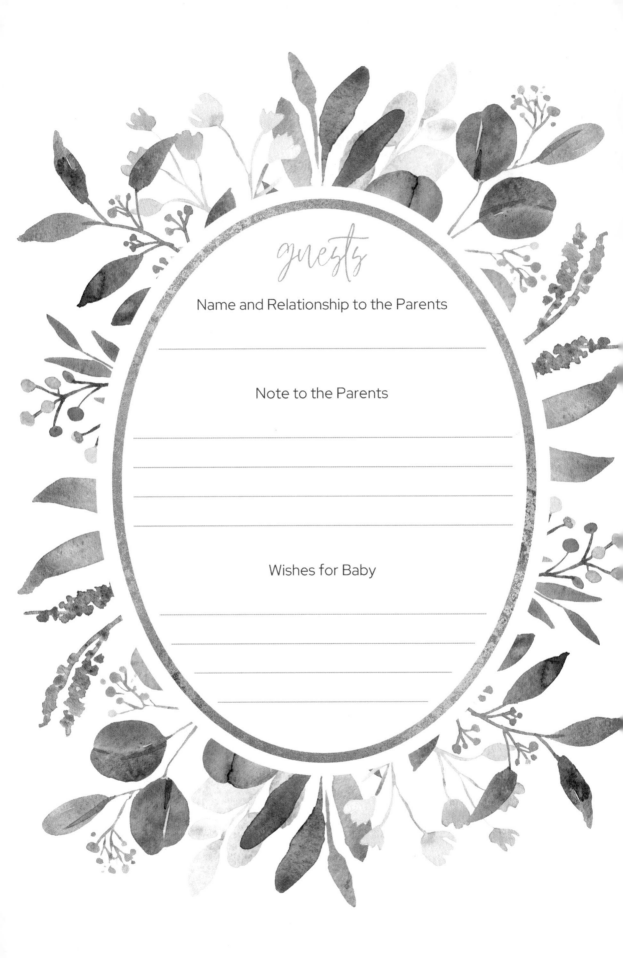

guests

Name and Relationship to the Parents

_____

Note to the Parents

_____
_____
_____
_____

Wishes for Baby

_____
_____
_____
_____

guests

Name and Relationship to the Parents

_____

Note to the Parents

_____
_____
_____
_____

Wishes for Baby

_____
_____
_____
_____

guests

Name and Relationship to the Parents

_____

Note to the Parents

_____
_____
_____
_____

Wishes for Baby

_____
_____
_____
_____

guests

Name and Relationship to the Parents

_____

Note to the Parents

_____
_____
_____
_____

Wishes for Baby

_____
_____
_____
_____

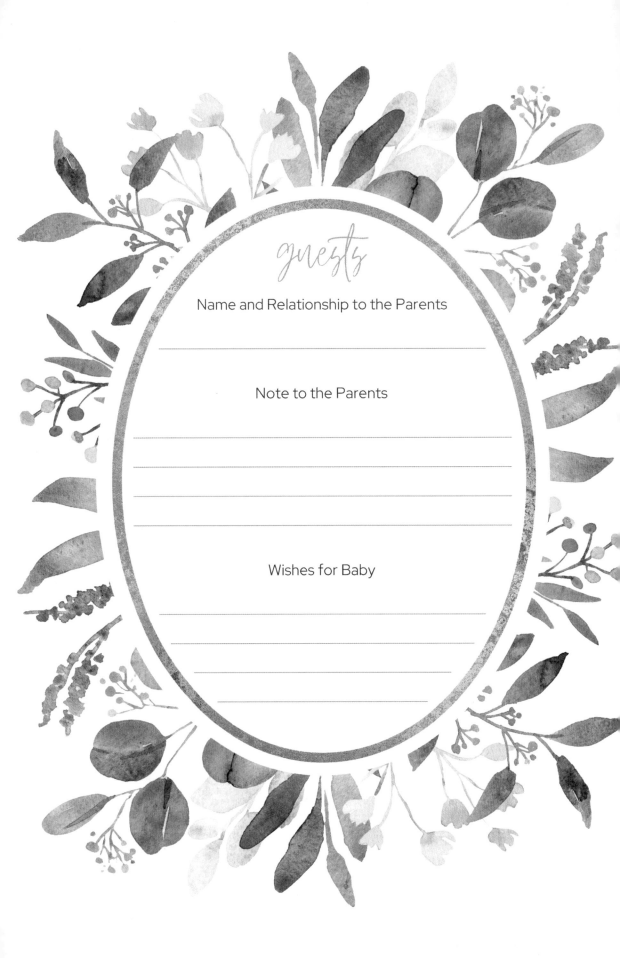

guests

Name and Relationship to the Parents

_____

Note to the Parents

_____
_____
_____
_____

Wishes for Baby

_____
_____
_____
_____

guests

Name and Relationship to the Parents

_____

Note to the Parents

_____
_____
_____
_____

Wishes for Baby

_____
_____
_____
_____

guests

Name and Relationship to the Parents

_____

Note to the Parents

_____
_____
_____
_____

Wishes for Baby

_____
_____
_____
_____

guests

Name and Relationship to the Parents

_____

Note to the Parents

_____
_____
_____
_____

Wishes for Baby

_____
_____
_____
_____

guests

Name and Relationship to the Parents

_____

Note to the Parents

_____
_____
_____
_____

Wishes for Baby

_____
_____
_____
_____

guests

Name and Relationship to the Parents

_____

Note to the Parents

_____
_____
_____
_____

Wishes for Baby

_____
_____
_____
_____

guests

Name and Relationship to the Parents

_____

Note to the Parents

_____
_____
_____
_____

Wishes for Baby

_____
_____
_____
_____

guests

Name and Relationship to the Parents

_____

Note to the Parents

_____
_____
_____
_____

Wishes for Baby

_____
_____
_____
_____

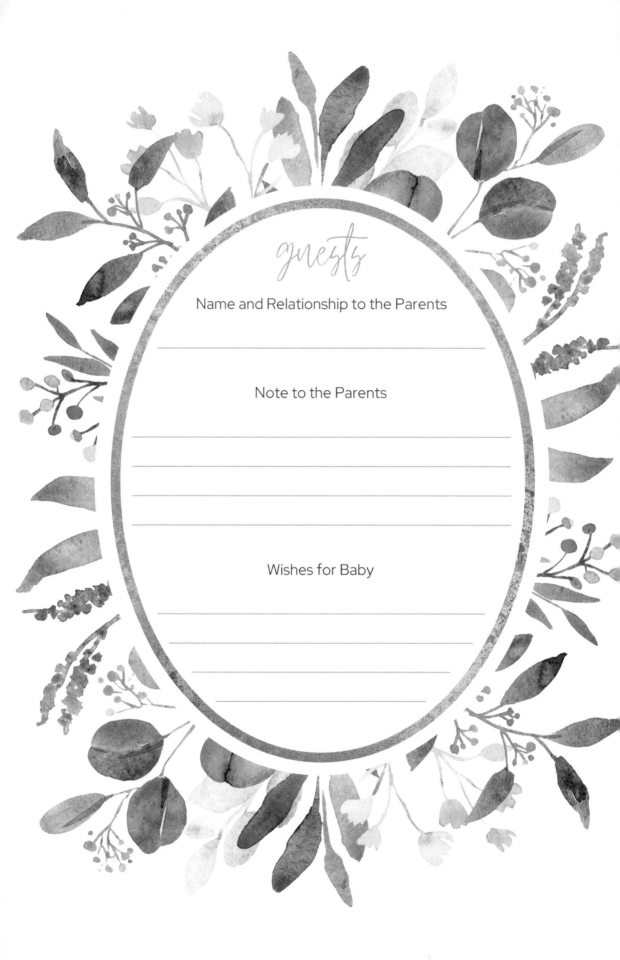

guests

Name and Relationship to the Parents

_____

Note to the Parents

_____
_____
_____
_____

Wishes for Baby

_____
_____
_____
_____

guests

Name and Relationship to the Parents

_____

Note to the Parents

_____
_____
_____
_____

Wishes for Baby

_____
_____
_____
_____

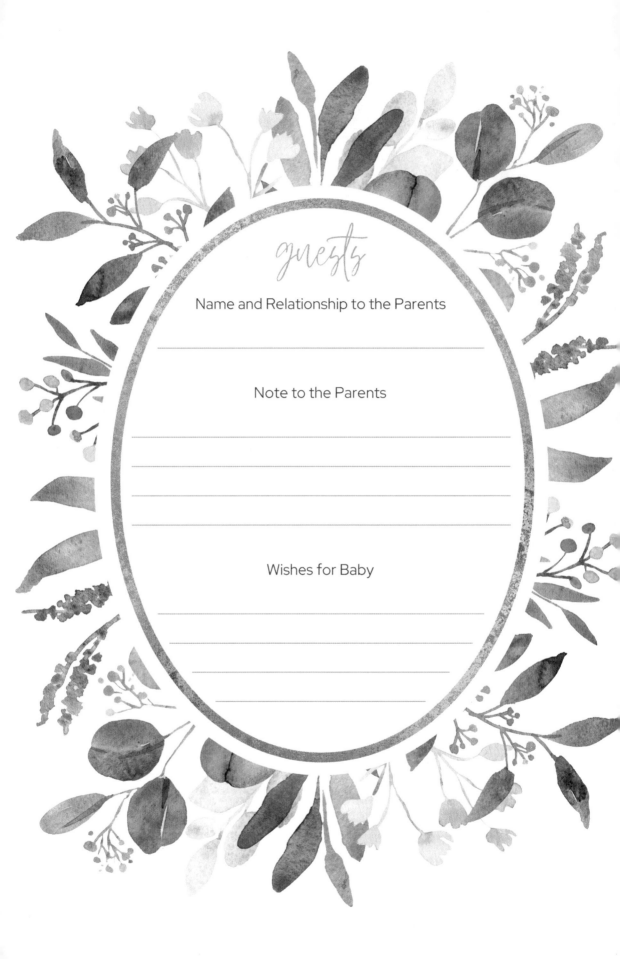

guests

Name and Relationship to the Parents

_____

Note to the Parents

_____
_____
_____
_____

Wishes for Baby

_____
_____
_____
_____

guests

Name and Relationship to the Parents

_____

Note to the Parents

_____
_____
_____
_____

Wishes for Baby

_____
_____
_____
_____

guests

Name and Relationship to the Parents

_____

Note to the Parents

_____
_____
_____
_____

Wishes for Baby

_____
_____
_____
_____

guests

Name and Relationship to the Parents

_____

Note to the Parents

_____

_____

_____

_____

Wishes for Baby

_____

_____

_____

_____

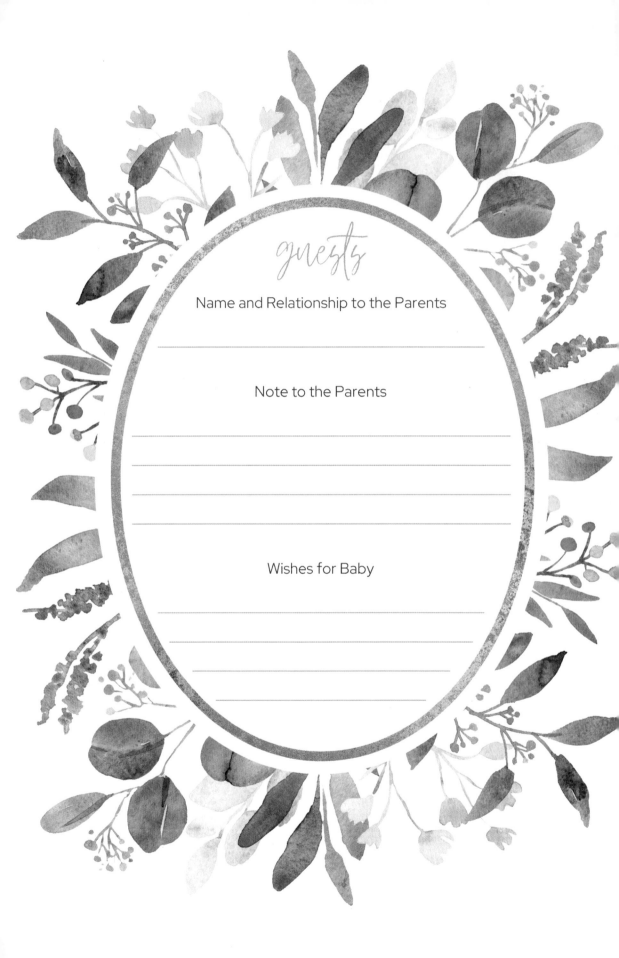

guests

Name and Relationship to the Parents

_____

Note to the Parents

_____
_____
_____
_____

Wishes for Baby

_____
_____
_____
_____

guests

Name and Relationship to the Parents

_____

Note to the Parents

_____
_____
_____
_____

Wishes for Baby

_____
_____
_____
_____

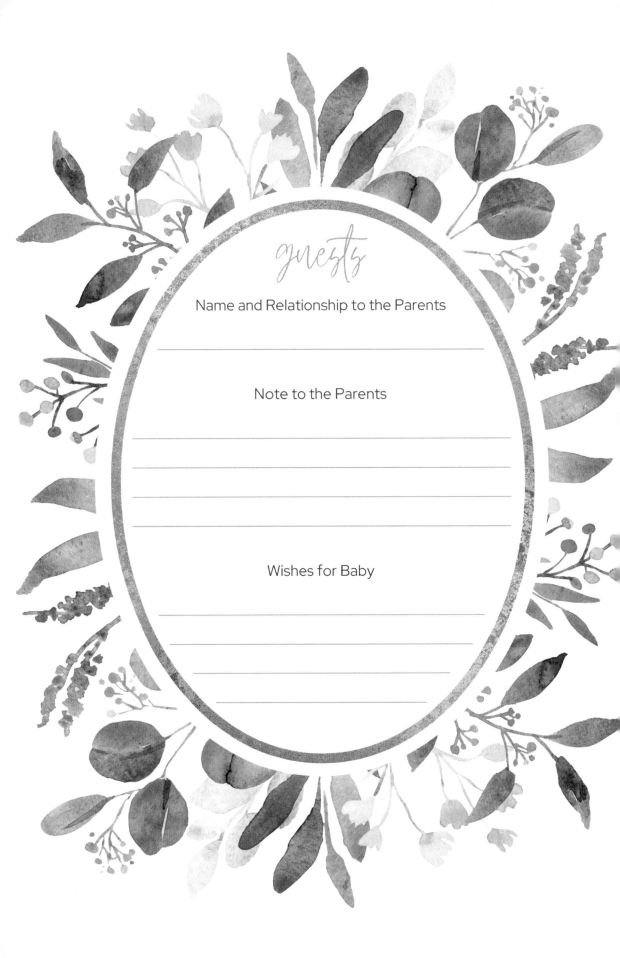

guests

Name and Relationship to the Parents

_____

Note to the Parents

_____
_____
_____
_____

Wishes for Baby

_____
_____
_____
_____

guests

Name and Relationship to the Parents

_____

Note to the Parents

_____
_____
_____
_____

Wishes for Baby

_____
_____
_____
_____

guests

Name and Relationship to the Parents

_____

Note to the Parents

_____
_____
_____
_____

Wishes for Baby

_____
_____
_____
_____

guests

Name and Relationship to the Parents

_____

Note to the Parents

_____
_____
_____
_____

Wishes for Baby

_____
_____
_____
_____

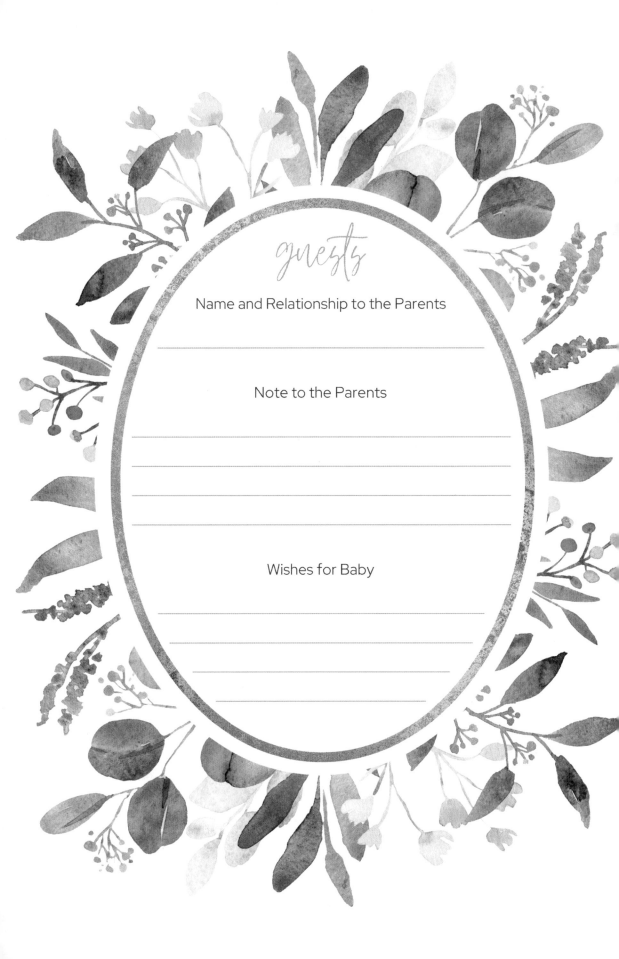

guests

Name and Relationship to the Parents

_____

Note to the Parents

_____
_____
_____
_____

Wishes for Baby

_____
_____
_____
_____

guests

Name and Relationship to the Parents

_____

Note to the Parents

_____
_____
_____
_____

Wishes for Baby

_____
_____
_____
_____

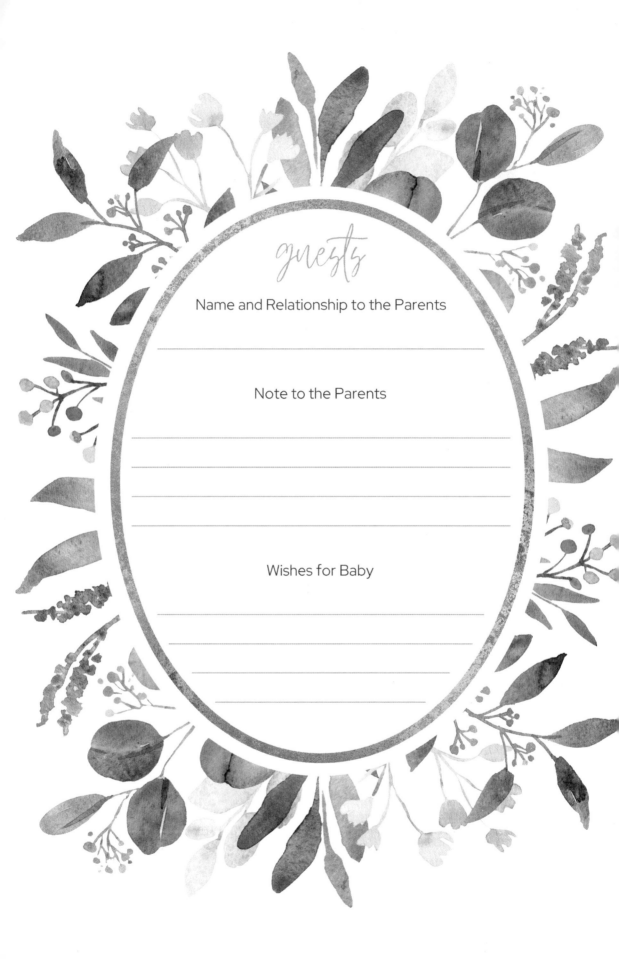

guests

Name and Relationship to the Parents

_____

Note to the Parents

_____
_____
_____
_____

Wishes for Baby

_____
_____
_____
_____

guests

Name and Relationship to the Parents

_____

Note to the Parents

_____
_____
_____
_____

Wishes for Baby

_____
_____
_____
_____

guests

Name and Relationship to the Parents

_____

Note to the Parents

_____
_____
_____
_____

Wishes for Baby

_____
_____
_____
_____

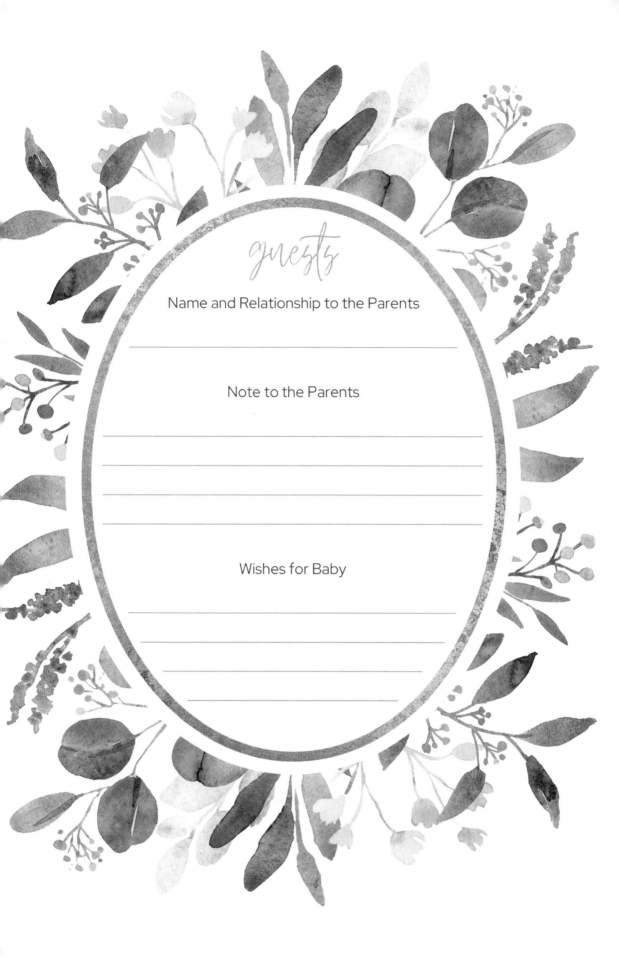

guests

Name and Relationship to the Parents

_____

Note to the Parents

_____
_____
_____
_____

Wishes for Baby

_____
_____
_____
_____

guests

Name and Relationship to the Parents

_____

Note to the Parents

_____
_____
_____
_____

Wishes for Baby

_____
_____
_____
_____

guests

Name and Relationship to the Parents

_____

Note to the Parents

_____
_____
_____
_____

Wishes for Baby

_____
_____
_____
_____

guests

Name and Relationship to the Parents

_____

Note to the Parents

_____
_____
_____
_____

Wishes for Baby

_____
_____
_____
_____

guests

Name and Relationship to the Parents

_____

Note to the Parents

_____
_____
_____
_____

Wishes for Baby

_____
_____
_____
_____

guests

Name and Relationship to the Parents

_____

Note to the Parents

_____
_____
_____
_____

Wishes for Baby

_____
_____
_____
_____

guests

Name and Relationship to the Parents

_____

Note to the Parents

_____
_____
_____
_____

Wishes for Baby

_____
_____
_____
_____

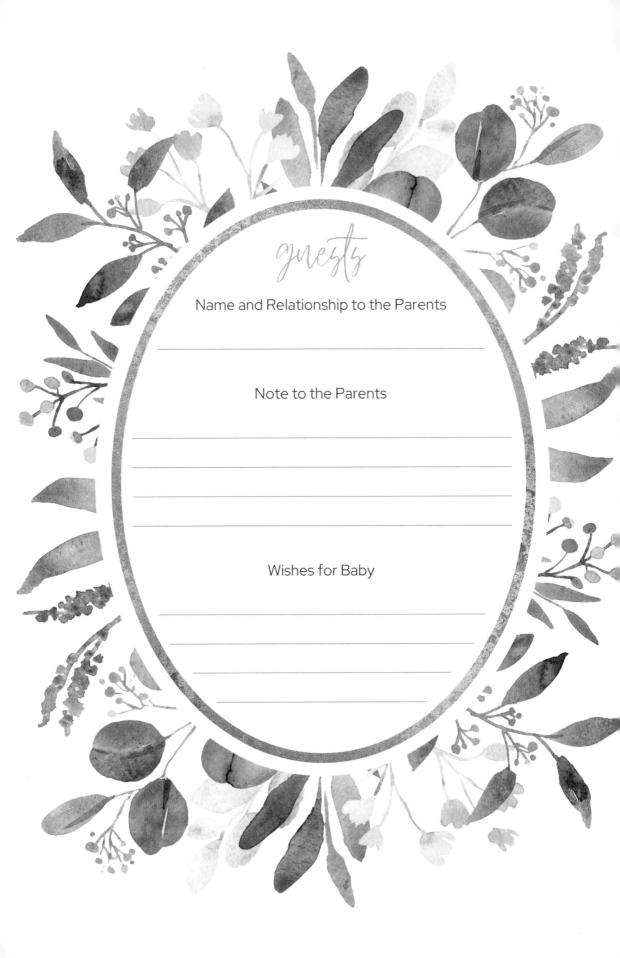

guests

Name and Relationship to the Parents

_____

Note to the Parents

_____
_____
_____
_____

Wishes for Baby

_____
_____
_____
_____

guests

Name and Relationship to the Parents

_____

Note to the Parents

_____
_____
_____
_____

Wishes for Baby

_____
_____
_____
_____

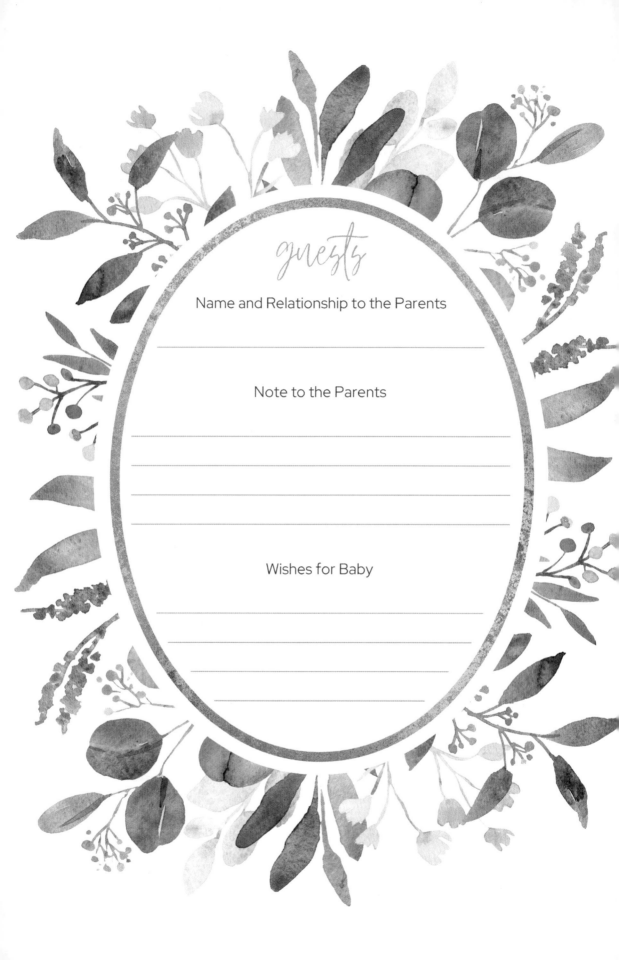

guests

Name and Relationship to the Parents

_____

Note to the Parents

_____
_____
_____
_____

Wishes for Baby

_____
_____
_____
_____

guests

Name and Relationship to the Parents

_____

Note to the Parents

_____
_____
_____
_____

Wishes for Baby

_____
_____
_____
_____

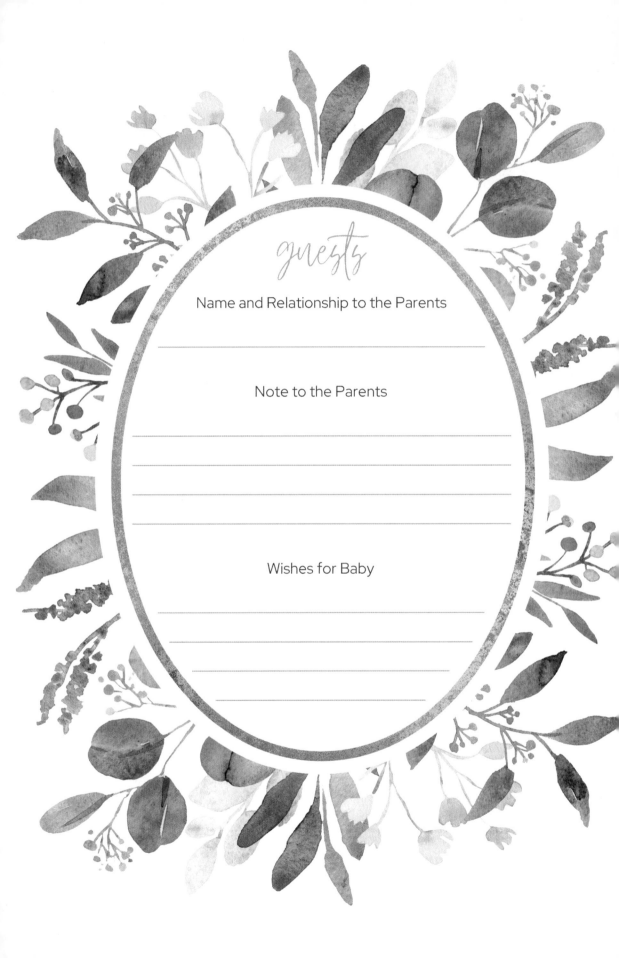

guests

Name and Relationship to the Parents

_____

Note to the Parents

_____
_____
_____
_____

Wishes for Baby

_____
_____
_____
_____

guests

Name and Relationship to the Parents

_____

Note to the Parents

_____
_____
_____
_____

Wishes for Baby

_____
_____
_____
_____

guests

Name and Relationship to the Parents

_____

Note to the Parents

_____
_____
_____
_____

Wishes for Baby

_____
_____
_____
_____

guests

Name and Relationship to the Parents

_____

Note to the Parents

_____
_____
_____
_____

Wishes for Baby

_____
_____
_____
_____

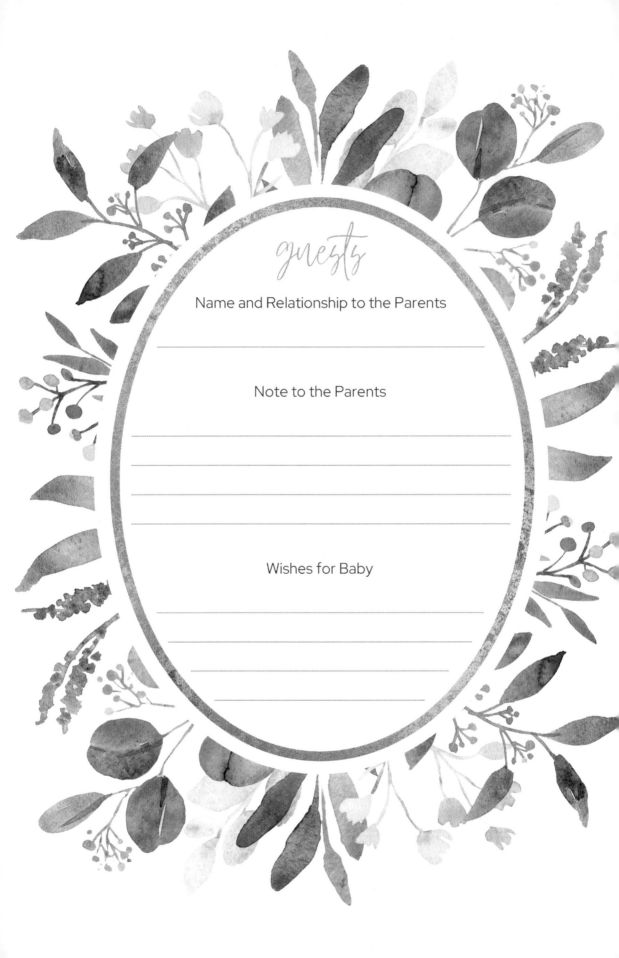

guests

Name and Relationship to the Parents

_____

Note to the Parents

_____
_____
_____
_____

Wishes for Baby

_____
_____
_____
_____

guests

Name and Relationship to the Parents

_____

Note to the Parents

_____
_____
_____
_____

Wishes for Baby

_____
_____
_____
_____

Gifts

Guest	Gift	Thank You Card Sent
		☐
		☐
		☐
		☐
		☐
		☐
		☐
		☐
		☐
		☐
		☐

Gifts

Guest	Gift	Thank You Card Sent
		☐
		☐
		☐
		☐
		☐
		☐
		☐
		☐
		☐
		☐
		☐

Gifts

Guest	Gift	Thank You Card Sent
		☐
		☐
		☐
		☐
		☐
		☐
		☐
		☐
		☐
		☐
		☐

Gifts

Guest	Gift	Thank You Card Sent
		☐
		☐
		☐
		☐
		☐
		☐
		☐
		☐
		☐
		☐
		☐

Gifts

Guest	Gift	Thank You Card Sent
		☐
		☐
		☐
		☐
		☐
		☐
		☐
		☐
		☐
		☐
		☐

Gifts

Guest	Gift	Thank You Card Sent
		☐
		☐
		☐
		☐
		☐
		☐
		☐
		☐
		☐
		☐
		☐

Gifts

Guest	Gift	Thank You Card Sent
		☐
		☐
		☐
		☐
		☐
		☐
		☐
		☐
		☐
		☐
		☐

Gifts

Guest	Gift	Thank You Card Sent
		☐
		☐
		☐
		☐
		☐
		☐
		☐
		☐
		☐
		☐
		☐

Gifts

Guest	Gift	Thank You Card Sent
		☐
		☐
		☐
		☐
		☐
		☐
		☐
		☐
		☐
		☐
		☐

Gifts

Guest	Gift	Thank You Card Sent
		☐
		☐
		☐
		☐
		☐
		☐
		☐
		☐
		☐
		☐
		☐

memories

memories

memories

memories

memories

memories

memories

memories

memories

memories

Made in the USA
Monee, IL
21 June 2022

d045c6ad-66f7-4229-8e7c-aebff61131c8R01